HEALTHY HABITS

EATING WELL

by Emma Carlson Berne

Consultant: Beth Gambro
Reading Specialist, Yorkville, Illinois

Minneapolis, Minnesota

Teaching Tips

Before Reading

- Look at the cover of the book. Discuss the picture and the title.

- Ask readers to brainstorm a list of what they already know about eating well. What can they expect to see in the book?

- Go on a picture walk, looking through the pictures to discuss vocabulary and make predictions about the text.

During Reading

- Read for purpose. Encourage readers to think about eating habits as they are reading.

- Ask readers to look for the details of the book. What are they learning about how to eat in a way that is healthy?

- If readers encounter an unknown word, ask them to look at the sounds in the word. Then, ask them to look at the rest of the page. Are there any clues to help them understand?

After Reading

- Encourage readers to pick a buddy and reread the book together.

- Ask readers to name two reasons to make healthy eating a habit. Find the pages that tell about these things.

- Ask readers to write or draw something they learned about eating well.

Credits:
Cover and title page, © karelnoppe/Shutterstock, © Pixel-Shot/Shutterstock; 3, © Mny-Jhee/Adobe Stock; 5, © Monkey Business/Adobe Stock; 6-7, © Tan Kian Khoon/Adobe Stock; 8-9, © Allistair F/peopleimages.com/Adobe Stock; 10-11, © Monkey Business Images/Shutterstock, © Trong Nguyen/Shutterstock; 13, © FG Trade Latin/iStock; 14-15, © mae_chaba/Shutterstock; 16-17, © Adisa/Shutterstock; 18-19, © GeorgiNutsov/iStock; 21, © Monkey Business Images/Shutterstock; 22T, © baibaz/Adobe Stock; 22M, © Africa Studio/Adobe Stock; 22B, © Pixel-Shot/Adobe Stock; 23TL, © Andrey/Adobe Stock; 23TM, © nukeaf/Shutterstock; 23TR, © Tatevosian Yana/Shutterstock; 23BL, © Allistair F/peopleimages.com/Adobe Stock; 23BM, © TinPong/Adobe Stock; 23BR, © SolStock/iStock.

STATEMENT ON USAGE OF GENERATIVE ARTIFICIAL INTELLIGENCE
Bearport Publishing remains committed to publishing high-quality nonfiction books. Therefore, we restrict the use of generative AI to ensure accuracy of all text and visual components pertaining to a book's subject. See BearportPublishing.com for details.

Library of Congress Cataloging-in-Publication Data

Names: Berne, Emma Carlson, 1979- author.
Title: Eating well / Emma Carlson Berne.
Description: Minneapolis, Minnesota : Bearport Publishing Company, [2024] |
   Series: Healthy habits | Includes bibliographical references and index.
Identifiers: LCCN 2023028236 (print) | LCCN 2023028237 (ebook) | ISBN
   9798889162421 (library binding) | ISBN 9798889162490 (paperback) | ISBN
   9798889162551 (ebook)
Subjects: LCSH: Nutrition--Juvenile literature. | Food habits--Juvenile
   literature.
Classification: LCC TX355 .B476 2024 (print) | LCC TX355 (ebook) | DDC
   641.3--dc23/eng/20230724
LC record available at https://lccn.loc.gov/2023028236
LC ebook record available at https://lccn.loc.gov/2023028237

Copyright © 2024 Bearport Publishing Company. All rights reserved. No part of this publication may be reproduced in whole or in part, stored in any retrieval system, or transmitted in any form or by any means, electronic, mechanical, photocopying, recording, or otherwise, without written permission from the publisher.

For more information, write to Bearport Publishing, 5357 Penn Avenue South, Minneapolis, MN 55419.

Contents

A Yummy Habit! 4

Make It a Habit 22

Glossary 23

Index 24

Read More 24

Learn More Online................. 24

About the Author 24

A Yummy Habit!

I bite into an apple.

Crunch!

I love this sweet treat.

It is good to eat fruit often.

I eat well to take care of myself.

It is something I do every day.

That makes it a **habit**!

I have three meals during the day.

Breakfast gets me ready in the morning.

Lunch keeps me going.

I eat dinner at night.

Having **regular** meals is part of eating well.

This keeps me full.

Sometimes, I get hungry between meals.

Then, I have a small snack.

I try to eat food that is good for me.

Lots of things have **protein**.

This helps my body grow strong.

Say protein like PROH-teen

The right food gives me **energy**, too.

Grains fill me up.

Then, I have power for my day.

I eat fruits and veggies that are many colors.

They are a part of every meal.

Fruits and veggies have many **nutrients** my body needs.

My body needs drinks, too.

When I am **thirsty**, I have water.

I drink milk sometimes, too.

Eating well makes me feel good.

It gives me energy every day.

I like to make it a healthy habit!

Make It a Habit

A habit is something you do every day. What are ways we can make eating well a habit?

Mornings are busy! Plan a healthy breakfast the night before.

When you pick your lunch, grab a fruit or veggie first. Then, choose the rest.

Do you want a snack? Have some fruit!

Glossary

energy the power to do things, such as work or run

habit something done regularly

nutrients parts of food that bodies use to stay alive

protein something in food that helps build strong bodies

regular happening over and over at the same time

thirsty feeling like you need to drink something

Index

breakfast 8, 22
dinner 8
fruit 4, 16, 22
grains 15
habit 6, 20, 22
hungry 10
lunch 8, 22
veggies 16, 22

Read More

Chang, Kirsten. *Eating Healthy (A Healthy Life)*. Minneapolis: Bellwether Media, 2022.

MacReady, R. J. *Eating Healthy Foods (Healthy Choices)*. New York: Cavendish Square Publishing, 2022.

Learn More Online

1. Go to **www.factsurfer.com** or scan the QR code below.
2. Enter **"Healthy Habits Eating"** into the search box.
3. Click on the cover of this book to see a list of websites.

About the Author

Emma Carlson Berne lives with her family in Cincinnati, Ohio. Sometimes, she has oatmeal for lunch!